Twisted Steel, Mangled Bumpers & Shattered Windshields

CRASH!

John Gunnell

©2006 Krause Publications

Published by

 krause publications

An Imprint of F+W Publications

700 East State Street • Iola, WI 54990-0001
715-445-2214 • 888-457-2873

Our toll-free number to place an order or obtain
a free catalog is (800) 258-0929.

Library of Congress Catalog Number: 2006932841

ISBN 13-digit: 978-0-89689-449-5
ISBN 10-digit: 0-89689-449-5

Designed by Kara Grundman
Edited by Brian Earnest

Printed in China

Acknowledgments

The majority of the photos in this book were taken by the late Rodman Bingham, an investigator and commercial photographer from Menlo Park, California. According to his daughter, Patrice Bingham Offenhauser, Rodman "had a police scanner speaker in every room of the house, and in his car — big sweeping antenna on the back. He even had a special headset speaker under his pillow. His ear would always be tuned to the squelching of several emergency stations — drove Mom and me crazy! If he heard a call about an accident, he'd leave the house, hop in his car, and often be one of the first on the scene. It wasn't so much being an 'ambulance chaser' as much as priding himself on having the first, and the best, photos of a crime or accident scene which could then be used in the newspaper or in court proceedings.

"My father saw many gruesome and sad human casualties at these accident scenes, and I can remember hearing him cry in the darkroom once at something he must have seen — I believe it involved a child hit on a bicycle. Yes, he did all his own darkroom work. He could have pictures developed and printed and up to the *San Francisco Chronicle* — an hour drive — by midnight to make the next morning's front page. He never photographed an accident scene for its exploitive or voyeuristic opportunities. He never took, or sold, pictures that were of a gruesome nature just for money. He was extremely professional, with an eye more towards the forensic aspect of an accident scene rather than the carnal."

We are pleased to share the Bingham family archive is this book.

A special word of thanks also goes out to old school car guy Rusty Herlocher of Pennsylvania, who also owns an extensive library of wreck photos and who generously contributed images to this work. Rusty's own book, *Vintage Car Wrecks*, published in 2003 by Krause Publications, features much of his amazing collection.

People Working at Car Crashes: Then and Now

By John Gunnell

When this book is promoted the ads may describe the accidents scenes as "interesting," "unusual" or "humorous." It's true that you can learn interesting things from these photos and that some of the cars wound up in unusual places. And there's a photo of a '56 Chevy in a sinkhole and a policeman smiling nearby.

However, there is nothing funny about car crashes. Accidents hurt people and cost them money. They interrupt normal life and cause a lot of hassles that no one needs. While that teeter-tottering '56 Chevy may look comical, someone may have been hurt and someone had to pay to get the car out of the hole.

When a crash takes place, lots of people get involved. Some get paid to help, others are volunteers (with professional-level training) and some simply get sucked into the accident by bad timing and terrible luck. For instance, "I was standing there minding my own when the car skidded and hit the hydrant in front of me. Then, I was pulling the driver out, while my brother ran to call the cops."

Bystanders who witness the accident may be the first to get involved. Some are fast thinkers who spring into action and save lives. Others stand around and get in the way of professional rescuers. Still others hurt themselves, creating a secondary emergency. Most try to help as much as they can until professional rescuers arrive. This is probably the smartest thing to do.

This book shows people involved in car crashes back in the '50s and '60s. You'll notice different roles they play and how some roles change in 50 years.

Bystander vs. Good Sam

In the rescue profession, bystanders who help are known as "Good Sams." Good Samaritan laws shield them from tort issues. With the rapid response that professional rescuers provide today, bystanders at auto accidents can often help most by getting professional help rolling.

Today, 911 emergency numbers and cell phones make it easier for Good Sams to help out. If you see an accident and have no rescue training, call for help as quickly as possible. Sound the alert before making any heroic efforts.

Dial "O" for Operator vs. Dial 911

In the '50s and '60s, the systems set up for getting police, fire and medical help to an accident scene were far less sophisticated than the "enhanced 911" networks we have today. Even rural areas now have high-tech call dispatch centers. These fully computerized operations rely on highly-trained dispatchers to protect and serve the public.They are a far cry from the ticker-tape alarm systems of the early 1900s and a big improvement over the fire-call boxes used in the '50s and '60s. The professionals at the call center need as much information as they can get to direct rescuers to the proper place. If you happen to witness a car crash and call it in, be sure to tell the dispatcher what happened, when it happened, where it happened, who it happened to, why you called and to what degree you think people may have been hurt.

First Aid vs. First Responder

"First responder" has different meanings. In a strict sense, the Good Sam who witnesses a car crash and tries to help is the first one to respond. In the '50s and '60s there was no nationwide first responder system. Today, most people think of the "first responder community" as including local police, firefighters and emergency medical professionals. During the mid-'70s, specific first responder guidelines were established. First Responders had to take a foundation course in emergency medicine developed by the U.S. Department of Transportation.

Starting in 1990, the National Highway Traffic Safety Administration created a National EMS Education and Practice Blueprint that led to national acceptance of the First Responder as a recognized level of care within emergency medical services. The ability to get trained people to an accident scene has certainly improved a great deal in 50 years.

Cop vs. Law Enforcement Professional

In the '50s and '60s, police work was not as sophisticated as today. Some agencies did not have two-way radios. The squad cars you'll see in the book from the San Francisco Bay area appear to be much better equipped than those in service in rural areas at the time. You will also notice Harley-Davidson police motorcycles in many photos. While great for weaving through traffic, the "cop bikes" could not get to a scene as fast as modern police officers do.

Today, police units are quick to arrive. They will often be the first rescuers to arrive with municipal vehicles and special equipment. Medical First Responders may be at work, but law enforcement's quick response is important. The police can deal with traffic, crowd control, calming down victims who qualify as "walking wounded," taking care of legalities, helping with first aid or CPR, restraining combative victims and investigating the causes of an auto accident.

Fireman vs. Firefighter

Five decades ago, a lot of fire trucks dated back to the 1930s. Photos inside show a the Palo Alto Fire Department open-cab pumper that was probably a 1940s truck. Such equipment wasn't as speedy – or as safe – as the fire engines used today. Firefighters used to "suit up" while hanging on the back of a truck. Today they are required to ride inside the truck and they are usually fully-geared and ready to roll when they arrive at a crash scene.

Modern firefighters may get to a car crash before or after the police, but differences in response time are usually a matter of straws. It doesn't take long to man several pieces of fire apparatus and get them rolling.

At the scene, firefighters may take over traffic control so police officers can attend to other matters. Some firefighters may be Emergency Medical Technicians or Paramedics and get involved in helping out with treatment.

Flammable liquids leaking from a car or truck may cause a fire or spill that firefighters have to deal with. Even a vehicle that doesn't burn or leak may need to be secured with cribbing so rescuers can enter it safely. Though not available back in the '50s and '60s, the Hurst Tool is a firefighter responsibility today.

Another big job for firefighters is clean up. Once the victims and vehicles are taken care of, the firefighters may spend hours sweeping glass, searching for debris, hosing down burning auto parts and working to re-open a closed highway.

Ambulance attendant vs. EMT/Paramedic

In the '50s and '60s, ambulance services used car-based ambulances. Load-and-Go techniques were employed to transport victims. Rescue squads then had a driver and one or more ambulance attendants who worked in the rear of the "rig." The emphasis was on getting the injured to a hospital fast. Other than basic first aid, little medical help was rendered in the ambulance.

Today highly-skilled EMTs and Paramedics crew very sophisticated truck-based ambulances. Crew members are cross-trained to do any job from driving to defibrillation. Lifesaving procedures can be carried out long before they get to a hospital. The level of EMT training has risen so high that many can practice advanced skills that only paramedics could do just a few years ago.

Tow truck guy vs. vehicle recovery professional

In the '50s and '60s, when a car got wrecked, the "tow truck guy" came out with a "wrecker" to haul it away. Most tow trucks were based on 3/4- and 1-ton trucks and had single- or double-boom wreckers designed to hook onto the front or rear of the damaged vehicle and pull it away.

Today tow trucks are classified as "recovery vehicles" and the drivers are highly-trained professionals, probably with training in first aid, hazardous materials and quick-clearance techniques. Likely to appear on the accident scene are tilt-bed or roll-back tow trucks that the vehicle will be hoisted onto. At a big wreck, you may even see a "rotator" truck with a giant crane that can hoist a semi truck high into the air. Things have changed in the towing industry, too.

Investigator vs. Accident Reconstructionist

In the '50s and '60s, accidents were investigated by policemen who measured skid marks and took photos. The photos in this book were taken by Rodman Bingham, a licensed private investigator. He worked for lawyers and insurance adjusters in Menlo Park, California.

The quality of his work suggests that he was a true expert in the careful assessment of car crashes.

Today those do such work are called motor vehicle accident reconstructionists. They investigate serious motor vehicle accidents. The type of investigation depends on the details of each accident. They collect evidence (skid marks and paint transfer for instance) and personal data (driver, passenger and vehicle information). The reconstructionist collates this data in the form of accident reports and scaled diagrams to "reconstruct" the entire event.

The Internet has many pages posted by professionals who do accident reconstruction work. There are even listings for special mathematic courses that concentrate on the math and physics involved in motor vehicle accidents. Even accident investigations have gone high-tech, but this book gives you a "crash course" on the way it used to be years ago.

(Author John Gunnell turned in his EMT badge in May 2005 after 25 years of midnight runs to car crashes and wrecks. His hat is off to the professionals who continue to help people through their dedicated work in the emergency services field. It's no picnic – but it has its rewarding moments.)

When this 1956 Chevrolet Two-Ten Sports Sedan four-door hardtop was forced from the highway by an unidentified car, the young couple inside plummeted down the steep, rocky mountain. A well-placed tree stopped the tumbling car just short of the raging river.
(Rusty Herlocher photo)

A Ford Starliner two-door hardtop left the road and shattered several makeshift guard posts before tumbling onto its roof. Note the International delivery truck in the background filled with milk cans. (Photo courtesy of Jack Frey.)

A 1960 Chevrolet Brookwood four-door station wagon demonstrates that it is far more appropriate to go over a bridge than under one. It's hard to figure how the car got in this position. (Rusty Herlocher photo)

School bus crashes make headlines today, but they're nothing new. This one took place on February 7, 1956 when a 20-year-old LaSalle Touring Sedan rammed the back of Las Lonitas School District's Bus No. 2. Chances are the old car lost its brakes, since it did quite a bit of damage to the bus's sturdy bumper. The students looking out the window may be hoping for a day off. Note that the bus's rear emergency exit is the double-handled window.

It looks like someone tried to play spin-the-bottle with a formerly beautiful '52 Ford. The Custom Tudor sedan's "gangster" whitewall wound up pointing to the sky and the car slid into a '39 Chrysler Royal parked nearby. As you can see, the Chrysler lost a headlight and suffered at least a dented left front fender. The left half of the hood it out of kilter, too. The Ford was only five years old when this occurred on a sunny day in July.

The jeweled octagonal sign says "STOP," but it appears that this 1939 Plymouth Custom four-door sedan didn't do so in time. The accident took place on March 15, 1957 at the intersection of Middle Ave. and El Camino Real in Menlo Park, California. The truck at the left in the photo looks like an emergency vehicle but is lettered "Redwood Ice Delivery." Behind the Plymouth is a neat-looking '53 Ford Customline Victoria V-8.

This postwar Dodge pickup ran into another jeweled stop sign on the 500 block on Glenwood Ave. in Menlo Park in October of 1948. Check out the strange "you're-on-Candid-Camera" look on the face of the investigating officer.

This Chevrolet coach "took it on the nose" after running through a wooden fence and down a steep embankment. As you can see, the accident literally "knocked the stuffing out" of the car's front seat. A hefty tow truck with a sturdy double-boom wrecker unit has been dispatched to the scene, but getting this Chevy back on its tires might take some bigger equipment. Onlookers have started gathering to watch the show.

A 1962 Chevrolet Bel Air two-door sedan looks like its driver apparently didn't read the "Bridge Is Out" sign. Actually, the driver drove down the bank on the work road and into the river until running out of luck at the middle pier. (Rusty Herlocher photo)

Here's one way to bend up an antenna and ruin good radio reception! Apparently it didn't take long to turn the Plymouth Special Deluxe Club Coupe into a 1 1/2-door model in a relatively severe crash that broke about all of the glass, except the car's right-hand vent window. We're guessing this is a '47 or '48 model, since the white beauty rings were added to the accessories list in 1947. Save those fog lamps – they're worth a bunch today!

A 1946-1948 Chevy Stylemaster four-door sedan and a 1951 Buick Super went dancing cheek-to-cheek on October 1, 1955. Though '51 and '52 Buicks look quite similar, the '51s use the shorter bumper guards, seen here, which bolt to the top of the bumper bar. The cars met at an intersection at the 200 block of Roosevelt Ave., probably in Redwood City, California. The newer Buick has snazzy two-tone paint and Buick's trademark rooftop radio antenna.

Hoods on some Buicks of the '40s and '50s could be lifted from either side or — as happened here to a 1947 model by accident – completely removed. In this case, a 1951 Nash Statesman Super did the honors and the big Buick seems to have suffered most in the deal. Peter's Fine Food Restaurant in the background served sea food when this accident occurred on February 22, 1955.

A 1963 Chevrolet II Nova 300 Series sedan knocked over a gasoline pump, shattered the storefront glass and damaged merchandise. The calamity started in the street in front of the Firestone store when the Nova collided with a truck, jumped the curb and proceeded into the station. The fire department covered the area with foam as a precautionary measure. (Rusty Herlocher photo)

This 1952 or 1953 Austin wagon was not merely sideswiped – it was knocked for a loop by a 1948 or 1949 Packard and wound up resting on the driver's side. It took a pair of wreckers to straighten out the mess, including the '54 Ford F-350 that can be seen beyond the Packard. This scene was snapped on January 27, 1957 in Redwood City, California.

A Cadillac sideswiped a 1946-1948 Plymouth sedan on a rain-slicked curve on April 17, 1955. Judging from the hard hats, two of the men rendering aid to the motorist came from the Dodge truck parked just around the curve. A Cadillac ambulance is on the scene ready to help out.

Clearing this scene required two tow trucks, the Dodge wrecker behind the Cadillac and a GMC wrecker dispatched by Huss Radiator Service, which is in front of the 1946-48 Plymouth.

This 1963 Chevrolet Nova 300 station wagon was an unwelcome visitor. The car burst through the end of a mobile home, shattered the wall, fixtures and furniture, including a bed in which the resident was sleeping, pinning her beneath the car. The sleeping victim, although badly shaken, was not seriously injured. (Rusty Herlocher photo)

Chevrolet made only 28,443 of these 1947 Fleetmaster convertibles, so it's a shame to see one that was involved in a crash with a 1957 Lincoln. The Chevy ragtop can easily be identified as a 1947 model because '46s had full belt line moldings and '48s had a T-shaped ornament at the center of the grille. The Lincoln (viewable behind the Chevy) was almost a brand new car as the accident happened on March 8, 1957.

A 1964 Buick LeSabre sedan was in no position to clear this ditch. (Photo courtesy of Jack Frey)

A Chevrolet ragtop and a Plymouth seem to have made an unscheduled visit to palmist Madame Marla on the evening of December 23, 1963. Too bad they didn't stop by earlier to have the future predicted, because this scene might have been avoided. Or maybe they should have stopped at Sentinel Car Service for a safety check. The trunk trim indicates the car nearest the cameraman is a 1949 Chevrolet Styleline Deluxe 2100 convertible.

This 1964 Chevrolet Bel Air four-door sedan was destroyed, as was the life of the driver. (Rusty Herlocher photo)

This 1949 Chrysler took a wicked hit from the side during a late-night drive. Considering that the photo was snapped at 1:25 a.m. on July 19, 1953, alcohol may have been a contributing factor.

Ford met Ford in this August 6, 1955 crash. The hood of the '49 Ford Custom Fordor sedan folded up pretty badly after the car broadsided the sun-visored 1953 Ford sedan on a California roadway. It appears bad brakes weren't to blame, since the older car left some fairly heavy skid marks on the pavement. It also wears several accessories like a chrome exhaust tip and venetian blinds.

A '49 Ford Custom convertible got a little bent out of shape in this crash. This model originally sold for $1,886 with a six or $1,949 with eight. The "8" on the grille spinner indicates this one had the flathead V-8. This accident took place January 8, 1957 and the Ford was worth only $150-$250 at the time so it probably wasn't fixed. The Marwais Steel Co. truck it collided with is pictured elsewhere in this book.

This crash on June 17, 1959 involved a 1949 Oldsmobile 76 Deluxe Club Sedan with fender skirts. The car had fastback styling and may have taken the "fast" part of the design description a little too literally. When the driver lost control, the car hit a pole and knocked down some traffic lights.

A 1973 Mercury Cougar hardtop coupe was crunched beneath a trailer after being abandoned along a busy highway. The truck driver lost control when he hit the brakes in an attempt to avoid hitting the Cougar. The quick stop caused the trailer to shift loads and tip, right on top of the very vehicle he was trying so hard to avoid. (Rusty Herlocher photo)

A frontal collision did damage to many of the front-end components of this 1949 Pontiac Streamliner Deluxe 8 Sedan-Coupe. The Streamliner name was used only on fastback models and station wagons in 1949. Deluxe versions had bright metal headlight doors and gravel shields. This "Poncho" was in nice condition for a 13-year-old car when the accident occurred on June 2, 1962. It was probably valued at under $100 at that time.

This 1949 Pontiac Chieftain Sedan-Coupe looks like it tried to get through the door to the men's room and didn't quite fit. A "Silver 8 Streak" script on the front fender indicates the reliable 248.9-cid Pontiac flathead straight eight is under its bent-up hood. Silver Streak is not a model name. It refers to the "waterfall" hood trim. However, it actually appeared on the cars in 1948 and 1949, causing some confusion over the correct nomenclature.

The license plate suggests that this 1950 Buick Roadmaster must have first been licensed in 1951, but this accident took place on October 29, 1955. In California, metal tabs were issued periodically to update the rear plates, but the front plates did not get new tabs and continued to show an older date — often that of the car's original registration. The license plate frame indicates the car was sold by Budd Buick of Burlingame, California.

A 1974 Chevrolet Caprice gave a 1980 Oldsmobile Cutlass a messy piggyback ride. (Photo courtesy of The Lock Haven Express)

A 1966 Ford Galaxie 500 four-door sedan was sitting in the wrong place when a trained dumped its load of coal. (Rusty Herlocher photo)

This forlorn-looking 1950 Cadillac Series 61 sedan is wearing a frown following a mishap in the middle of the street. The beat-up Caddy is still waiting for a wrecker to drag it off the busy four-lane divided road.

This vintage Model T center door sedan drew a crowd of you onlookers after a bumpy ride in an urban area. The rear passenger side wheel is definitely going to need some attention.

We don't know the name of the street that this '46 Studebaker Club Coupe rolled over on, but the house number on the mailbox crushed under the car is 282. It didn't take long for the "Neighborhood Investigative Team" to arrive by bicycle and check out the situation. Overall, the car doesn't look like it was damaged too badly, but the occupants of the Studebaker must have been quite shaken up.

Did you ever notice how wrecks seem to attract wreckers? This "Pilothouse" Dodge AAA double-boom Emergency truck has a Chrysler product on the hook, while the owner of the damaged 1950 Chevrolet Styleline Deluxe two-door sedan has to wait for his tow to arrive. The Dodge wrecker was dispatched from "Miles Ahead" Miles Motors in Redwood City, California.

It looks like someone lost control of this 1950 Ford Fordor sedan and ran into a restaurant or café. The crash ruined some cactus plants and left quite a mess. This accident occurred on February 2, 1960. The teenagers eyeballing the front end damage to the car must have been fans of the television series "77 Sunset Strip." The boy in the light jacket, especially, has the "Kookie" look popularized by actor Ed Byrnes.

This photo was taken in Sheboygan, Wisconsin, on May 20, 1937. It shows Elmer Nordness proudly posing with an unidentified vehicle that somehow wound up perched on its side in the middle of the street.

A 1955 Oldsmobile Super 88 four-door sedan went through a red light and thrashed an unsuspecting 1951 Chevrolet Styleline Special.
(Rusty Herlocher photo)

Here's a wrecked car that would definitely be restored today. The 1950 Ford Custom Deluxe 8 convertible coupe ran afoul of a 1955 Chevrolet Bel Air four-door sedan. A couple of kids are having fun checking out the carnage.

This officer must have been "point person" on the accident investigation team. Something about the 1950 Packard's broken rear window has caught his attention. Beginning October 1, 1949 the 23rd Series "Golden Anniversary" Packards — like this one — were designated 1950 models for registration purposes. At almost the same time, Ultramatic Drive was introduced.

If your '50 Plymouth Special Deluxe sedan is going to crash, it might just as well happen at the city limits so you get lots of first responders rolling to help you out. This crash occurred on May 26, 1959.

A Model T sedan got this worst of this encounter with a vintage Studebaker (left). These beautiful old cars were not built to survive even modest impacts like this.

This bullet-nose '50 Studebaker is a Regal Deluxe model with chrome-plated headlight housings. The car that it ran into is a '55 Ford Customline. The large badge on the front bumper is from the National Automobile Club. Headquartered in Foster City, California, the National Automobile Club has provided reliable emergency roadside assistance to motorists since 1924.

The roof of this 1950 Studebaker Land Cruiser is bent up pretty badly, but as you can see it did not collapse in what looks like a severe rollover-type accident. This 124-inch-wheelbase model was merchandised as a sub-series of the Commander. It sold for $2,187 when new and 24,712 were built. The chrome headlight housings seen here were a running change in standard equipment.

Here's one way to create excitement in a normally sleepy neighborhood. An AAA wrecker is on the scene getting ready to haul away a 1951 Buick that ran into the 1956 Chevy in the background. The wrecker – parked just behind the Buick – is a "Task Force" style GMC operated by Crestwood Pontiac, a dealership once located at the intersection of Alma and Forest in Palo Alto, California. The date of this crash was May 4, 1957.

The driver of this 1951 Chevy Special Six two-door sedan was very lucky the car stopped when it did. A dented rear fender is a lot better than rolling down an embankment. The driver of a '41 Ford truck has stopped to check things out.

If you can determine that this was an early Hudson, probably a 1914-15, then you know your Hudsons. This one obviously lost a battle with a train.

It appears the curb helped trip up this Model T, which wound up on its side, to the fascination of a large group of bystanders.

The two-tone 1954 Chrysler Newport hardtop on the left seems to have had a big fender bender with a stately looking 1951 or 1952 Imperial Newport hardtop. The signs in the background say "one way" and "stop," but it might be that one of these cars was going the wrong way and the other didn't stop.

Something heavy crushed this T from what appears to be the cowl back. It was relegated to the junkyard.

Roller skating can be a dangerous pastime, and not only due to the chance of falling flat on your face. These derby damsels ran into something on their way home from the rink and dented up their 1951 Dodge Wayfarer coupe. The car is one of only 6,702 built. In the background behind the car is the Mercantile Acceptance Company where G.I. Loans were available to World war II Vets.

Here's another look at this "roller derby" pileup. This crash took place on February 15, 1957. A 1951 Buick Super four-door sedan complete with Dynaflow Drive tangled with the Dodge.

This once-splendid 1966 Mustang wound up parked in the wrong place when a earthquake hit.

Shoebox Fords were a favorite of West Coast hot rodders and customizers. This 1951 Custom Deluxe convertible has a continental tire kit and a hopped-up look about it. Unfortunately, it wasn't quite fast enough to get out of the way of whatever hit it. The accident took place on January 21, 1958. The Official Automobile Guide *of that year lists values of $230-$405 for a seven-year-old Ford convertible.*

Featuring Chrysler Corporation's well-known "box-on-box" postwar styling, this 1951 Plymouth two-door sedan was only five years old when it met its doom on California Highway 101. A close look with a magnifying glass shows it to have completely bald front tires, so an accident may have been waiting to happen. The damage was caused by a crash with a 1950 Ford.

This 1947 Chevy ragtop got tangled up with some sturdy cement pylons and a may also have clipped a sign post in this July 26, 1955 mishap.

Firefighters didn't arrive in time to save this vintage VW bug from having a total meltdown in this 1965 incident. The Beetle appears to have come off the dirt embankment to the left and wound up capsized.

A pretty 1955 Mercury Montclair two-door hardtop has hit an early 1950s Studebaker on a rainy night.

Hugging a lamppost like "Freddie the Freeloader" — a tipsy character created by comedian Red Skelton — this '52 Ford Crestline Sunliner looks a little helpless. Though not quite a rare car when new, with production of 22,534 units, such a ragtop is certainly very collectible today. The convertible was a V-8 only model and used Ford's 239-cid/101-hp flathead V-8 to get around. This one was worth $400-$600 when the March 19, 1958 crash occurred.

"C'mon guys, get those hands out of your pockets and give me a little push," says the '52 Ford convertible also seen in the previous photo. As you can tell in this view, the car didn't impact the lamp post head-on. It was probably sliding out of control to the left when it hit against the "immovable object." There's plenty of damage to the fender parts, hood and grille. In addition, some front suspension damage is likely, too.

Both front fenders and the entire grille assembly seem to be missing from this 1962 Cadillac Coupe DeVille after a June 13, 1962 accident. All 1952 Cadillacs were anniversary models honoring the automaker's 50th year in business. To celebrate, the cars had special gold-finished V-8 emblems and gold ornaments on a plate below the headlights. This hacked up hardtop has lost all its "jewelry" in the nasty accident.

This must be a 1952 MG TD roadster because it has both "dished" style dashboard gauges and rectangular tail lights. The dish-faced speedometer and tachometer were used in production from October 1951-1953. A car built in October 1951 probably would have been licensed here as a '52 model and the '53 TD had round tail lights. The May 6, 1956 accident really did a number on the Auster windscreen. Note the gas leaking from the flip-up filler cap.

An old Chevrolet (left), a Packard (right) and what appears to be a Ford (center) combined to form one big mass of twisted metal after this May 1954 wreck.

The "little Nash Rambler" got a little banged up by a big tree. Well, maybe it's not a really big tree, but it probably seemed like it was to the 176-inch-long Rambler station wagon. For 1952, the Greenbrier wagon was upgraded with two-tone paint and richer trim. As you can see, even in the '60s, California did not issue update stickers for front license plates – only rear ones.

In a typical early-'60s Haz-Mat response, a firefighter flushes fluids spilled in a two-car crash off the road. He is near a '52 Plymouth Special Deluxe four-door sedan that ran into a '55 Pontiac. The '52 Plymouth has distinct stone shields and a model name in script on the front fender. The street sign pinpoints the location as El Verano, which is a Census Designated Place (CDP) in Sanoma County, California. The accident occurred on December 4, 1960.

It doesn't appear that the '59 Chevrolet panel truck in the background was involved in this crash, but the '52 Ford Customline V-8's bent fender and the '53 Buick Roadmaster sedan with its "headlight punched out" certainly were. The Roadmaster also lost a couple of "teeth" in the incident that took place February 9, 1961. In the Super, Century and Roadmaster series, 1953 was the maiden year for a Buick V-8 engine.

It looks like traffic was backed up pretty badly by this August 14, 1955 crash involving a 1953 Chevrolet Two-Ten two-door sedan and a nearly new 1955 Ford two-door Ranch Wagon. The Ford was purchased at Towne Ford in Redwood City, California. Towne Ford Sales & Leasing is still the franchised Ford dealer in Redwood City today. It is located at 1601 El Camino Real.

What looks like a pretty nice 10-year-old 1953 Buick Roadmaster probably took its last ride on March 11, 1963. Founded in 1903, Buick Motor Division celebrated its "Golden Anniversary" in 1953 and built some fine automobiles. Too bad this one lasted only a decade.

This 1953 Ford probably hit a prewar or early postwar coupe, which appears through its rear window, before running into a gnarly tree. It took a hit on the right front fender and the hood, grille and bumper are twisted up a bit. The tag topper on the 1951 California commercial license plate indicates the car was purchased at S & C Motors. The date of the crash was February 20, 1955.

What appears to be a 1953 De Soto Powermaster (left) collided with a 1951 Chevrolet near some type of rural embankment.

"Ooouch!" might have been uttered by the Voice of the West after this crash on the evening of October 14, 1957. We're guessing that truck No. 44 in the San Francisco Chronicle's *newspaper delivery fleet was a 1953 GMC 1-ton Panel Delivery.*

With dual spotlights, painted headlight doors, "bottle cap" hubcaps and the full factory police package, this '53 Oldsmobile 88 was not a car you wanted to see in your rearview mirror half a century ago. It was part of the California Highway Patrol fleet until this March 13, 1954 crash with a telephone pole. It appears to be a stick-shift model, which made a very neat combination with the 165-hp four-barrel version of the 303-cid Olds Rocket V-8.

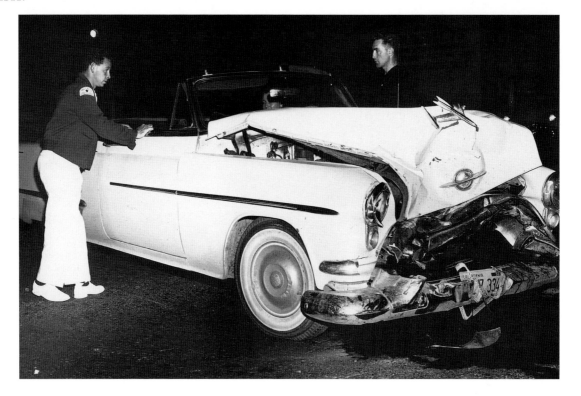

Here's another rare ragtop that probably never made it to a car show or cruise night. The '53 Oldsmobile Super 88 convertible coupe really "took it on the chin" when it crashed into another car on May 24, 1956 near Palo Alto, California. This car cost $2,615 when new and was one of just 8,310 made. It was powered by the 303-cid/165-hp Rocket V-8. A member of the Palo Alto Ambulance Service is leaning on the door and talking to the driver.

This 1953 Plymouth Cambridge Club Coupe suffered extensive right front damage in a February 4, 1957 highway accident. Believe it or not, this is quite a rare automobile. The Cambridge Club Coupe sold for $1,707 when it was new and only 1,050 were made. It was powered by a 217.8-cid/100-hp flathead six. In addition to being rare, it was also a 25th anniversary model, since Plymouth started producing cars in 1928.

Anyone who thinks of '53 Plymouths as "cheaply made little cars" might want to find and talk to the driver of the 1956 Studebaker truck that met this Cambridge four-door sedan at the intersection of Oberlin and College in Menlo Park, California. The crash that took place January 11, 1958.

In this crash one of America's earliest compact cars had the misfortune of running into one of its top luxury cars. The 1953 Willys Aero Lark two-door sedan was only 181 inches long and weighed just 2,487 lbs. In contrast, the black 1951 or 1952 Cadillac was about 212 inches long and about 1,500 lbs. heavier. Note the unusual close-together positioning of the Willys' door handle and window crank.

This '54 Cadillac with dual spotlights suffered a black eye and busted lip in this tussle with another vehicle. These two-door beauties are definite collector prizes today. This one was beat up, but not totalled. It might still be on the road somewhere.

You can see lots of old trucks, a Ford woodie and a Cadillac ambulance in this scene of an accident that happened on August 12, 1955. The damaged Buick is one of only 6,135 Special convertibles made in 1954. It was only a year old and looks to be in great condition.

A utility pole seems to be growing out of the middle of a mangled 1940 Plymouth, which crashed near a night club in June 1953.

This 1957 Plymouth Belvedere Sport Suburban was involved in the "St. Valentine's Massacre" on February 14, 1957. The almost-new station wagon seems to have hit a 1956 Chevy. It is surrounded by other Chevys including 1955 and 1957 police cars. Our friends from Lloyd's 24-Hour Towing Service are getting ready to position the wrecker to haul the car away. Be careful guys — don't bump into that police department Harley-Davidson Servi-Car!

Check out the crazy configuration of this Chevy pickup's front bumper after this utility pole refused to yield. A dog on the other side of the fence seems to have been a witness to the accident.

This 1956 Volkswagen Beetle sedan got scrunched and crunched on February 3, 1958. This was one well-equipped Beetle with its white sidewall tires and radio and antenna. Fenders on these imports were bolt-on items and easy to replace. A new one, plus a new hood and bumper could put this "Bug" back on the road. Passing by in the background are a 1956 Mercury Montclair and a 1948 Studebaker Commander.

"Car 503, where are you?" In this case the City of Palo Alto squad car — a 1958 Ford Custom 300 four-door sedan — butted heads with a 1952 Ford convertible. It's likely that taxpayers seeing the city's near-new cruiser in this condition weren't very happy. The date of the accident was March 19, 1958.

A two-year-old 1956 Oldsmobile Ninety-Eight Holiday Sedan and a near-new Corvette bumped into each other at an intersection near the Bayshore Freeway around Menlo Park, California on July 7, 1958. After the impact, both GM cars wound up pointing in the same direction.

This 1955 Chevrolet Bel Air convertible was demolished and two were seriously injured in an early morning crash that happened directly across the street from a city hospital. Shattered glass from the Chevy's windows was embedded in the tree trunk. Note the factory wire wheel covers. (Rusty Herlocher photo)

A now-very-collectible 1957 Buick Caballero station wagon rammed this Rambler and pushed it into a hedge on Louis Boulevard in Palo Alto, California. Police motorcycle No. 507 responded to the crash and dispatched a tow truck from Crestwood Pontiac to the scene. The 1958 Rambler Super Sedan took heavy damage to its left-hand side and lost its wheel cover in the September 26, 1958 accident.

The Model T Ford on the right came out the loser of this conflict with an unidentified touring car on the left. With open cars like this and no visibility problems, it's hard to imagine why these two cars wound up running into each other nearly head-on. (Courtesy of Allister Fame)

An unfortunate 1954 Ford Customline two-door sedan V-8 was harpooned by a bridge railing when the driver tried to make a lane change. (Rusty Herlocher photo)

In late-1950s accidents — such as this crash on June 30, 1959 — it was common to see foreign cars tangled up with good old American iron. The Tudor sedan facing the camera is a decade-old 1949 Ford. The squarish, two-toned vehicle is a 1958 Volvo PV445 Duet station wagon. A shop-coated serviceman from Crestwood Pontiac is clearing the scene for recovery work.

Lloyd's 24-HR Towing of Palo Alto sent a new 1959 Ford F-250 tow truck to pick up a damaged 1959 Ford Custom 300 sedan. Both vehicles were very new, since the date of the accident was October 31, 1959. Happy Halloween – not!

It's hard to tell what make of car this is — probably a Chevrolet or Pontiac — but it definitely stopped abruptly when it ran into this house. The impact shoved the rear edge of the hood right through the windshield.

The responding police car in the background is a 1959 Chevrolet sedan put in service by the Menlo Park Police Department, so we assume that the smashed 1959 Ford Custom 300 squad car may belong to the same service. Note the E-encased-in-octagon California license plate, which was used on city and county exempt vehicles in the state. The police officer nearest the camera has his own Mamiya Flex camera.

The driver of this delivery truck was going to have some explaining to do to his insurance company after this crazy chain-reaction fender bender that involved five parked cars. This incident happened in California. (Courtesy of Michael E. Ware/Crummett Collection)

Peninsula British Cars was a popular dealer in Palo Alto and appears in photos in this book. The sports car nearest the camera — an MGA roadster — came from their inventory. The Triumph TR-2 may have, but we can't say for sure because its front license plate has been knocked off. All of the cars behind the Triumph were damaged in this chain-reaction crash in Redwood City.

Mercedes meets Mopar. In this particular case, it appears that the pointy-fendered '59 Plymouth won the battle as it has hardly any noticeable damage other than bent bumper guards, a ding in the bumper end and some minor dings in the headlight trim piece. In contrast, the classic Mercedes grille shell is twisted like a pretzel and the hood, fenders and bumpers are bent out of shape.

In the late 1950s, the U.S. economy suffered a recession and interest in inexpensive, economical cars made overseas exploded for a while. Of course more of these imports — like this 1959 Triumph Sedan Estate Wagon — got involved in accidents. This one occurred on April 10, 1962.

This amazing scene looks like something staged for a movie. Somehow, a 1950 Chevy Styline sedan wound up perched atop a partially overturned 1954 MG-TF roadster. Seeing as the MG-TF was not a particularly rugged car, there was no question who the winner would be if these two models tangled. (Courtesy of National Motor Museum of Great Britain)

This 1960 Cadillac Deville six-window sedan hit an early '61-63 Rambler American convertible on March 27, 1965. For a tiny squirt, the "Little Nash Rambler" did a bunch of damage to the big 225-inch-long Caddy. The AMC product weighed about 2,700 lbs. compared to 4,800 lbs. for the Cadillac.

A '51 Pontiac Chieftan convertible shook the leaves right out of this tree on March 1, 1953. The windshield glass wound up spread all over the ragtop and even the trunk.

It appears at first glance that the front end damage to this Triumph TR4 was minimal, but the ragtap was a casualty — presumably torn up to help extricate the occupants of the car.

This 1960 Oldsmobile Dynamic 88 ex-four-door sedan (now a three-door) was involved in a crash with a 1965 Ford police car on Pearl Harbor Day — December 7 — in 1965.

The Morris 1000 series was popular all over the world in the 1950s and many are restoring the cars today. The seat probably was removed when the driver was extricated.

If there was water in the culvert, you might guess that this car tried to become a "surfin' Safari." But the culvert was bone dry when the 1960 Pontiac Safari station wagon crashed and wound up in it. The date was October 8, 1963. There was a lot of heavily twisted metal on the car's left side, but it looks like the occupants were able to get out the other side.

This 1960 Pontiac Ventura Vista hardtop (Pontiac's name for its "flat-roof" four-door hardtop that year) put a pretty big dent in a 1954 Oldsmobile 88 four-door sedan, before the older car rolled on its side. But the traffic light on a pole didn't topple quite as easily. This accident took place on May 14, 1960 when the Pontiac was just about brand new.

This accident, on February 20, 1964, took place in front of a hospital. A sign notes that only physician's cars and ambulances are permitted to park there, so it probably didn't take long for medical help to arrive. The '61 Ford Fairlane four-door sedan absorbed a pretty devastating frontal impact.

Ford offered both two- and four-door Ranch Wagons in 1961. This one is the four-door model. This one was involved in an accident with a truck that overturned. The damage to the vehicle's right rear section included a broken window, a twisted bumper and a bent tail light.

In the early '60s American automakers countered a wave of imported cars with their own compacts. Oldsmobile's new-for-1961 small car was the F-85. Four station wagons were offered and this looks like the Deluxe five-passenger edition. It appears to have been hit by a motorcycle in the background.

Three onlookers take a close look at the front end damage suffered by this 1951 DeSoto Sportsman after its driver couldn't avoid a utility pole. The impact knocked out a few of the DeSoto's trademark "teeth" in the grille.

This accident took place on May 23, 1962. The 1961 Biscayne sedan put in service by the Menlo Park, California Police Department suffered extensive frontal damage. The car toppled a traffic light and a Walk/Don't Walk sign before ending what may have been its last ride. It suffered extensive frontal-impact damage.

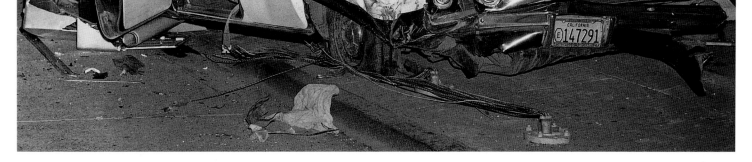

This 1960 Chevy squad car is in need of backup after jumping the curb and taking out a light pole in this May, 1963 accident. The pole is still pinned under the front end of the car and the wiring is strewn under the flat left rear tire.

Judging from many of these crash photos, big and small vehicles didn't get along well when small cars first started to become popular. This 1962 Corvair Monza Deluxe coupe was scrunched beyond repair by a huge dump truck. The bucket seat Monza was the most popular Corvair. It sold for $2,275 in 1962 and 151,738 were made. This one was 10 years old when it got involved in this July 24 crash.

About all the was left of the Corvair was it its rear-mounted engine, which seems to have been mostly unscathed by this ugly encounter.

It's hard to imagine how this 1942 Chevy wound up balancing on the hood of a parked '40 Plymouth. The Chevy suffered some damage to the roof on the driver's side, but how it wound up climbing atop the Plymouth is anybody's guess. The Plymouth seems to be holding up well — the impact didn't even break a headlight!

This May 9, 1964 accident involved a 1963 Dodge 440 two-door hardtop that encountered what looks like a Ford model on a busy California highway. It looks like a fender bender, but damage to the roof of the FoMoCo car makes it seem that it flipped over. Crowd control at the scene looks kind of lax, with kids, bicycles and even a dog milling about. One of the cars up the road on the other side of the street is a new Pontiac GTO.

Here's one to drive a Barrett-Jackson auction-goer crazy. That's a just-about-mint and almost-brand-new '65 Pontiac GTO convertible that the tow truck is rigging up to pull. Lots of damage to this "Gran Turismo Omologato," including an out-of-kilter fender, a bumped bumper, a haunched hood and a "see-through" windshield. How do you like the tow truck operator's tight "pegged" pants. They were all the rage back in the '60s.

It's obvious this huge '56 Buick went up in flames after it was hammered from behind by a truck. A firefigher with the No. 1 on his helmet is still on the scene, hosing down the smoldering wreck.

Wrecks, Wrecks and More Wrecks!

More than 400 post-accident images from the 50s, 60s and 70s will have you wincing and maybe even gripping your own steering wheel just a little bit tighter, while anecdotal and informative captions provide you with relevant model and technical information.

You'll see the automobile industry's progress in the development and implementation of mandatory and voluntary safety features throughout the years as revealed through the evolution of safety standards that affected the design, styling, and engineering of the cars we drive today.

So fasten your seatbelt and enjoy this *"sometimes bumpy"* ride through time.

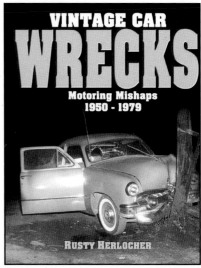

VINTAGE CAR WRECKS
Motoring Mishaps
1950 - 1979
RUSTY HERLOCHER

Softcover • 8-½ x 11 • 224 pages
400 b&w photos
Item# AW03 • $19.99

There were 11,950 of these Holiday Sedans built in 1955. This one took the plunge on May 2, 1961. We're guessing nobody used the diving board for at least a couple days.

This Oldsmobile Super 88 Holiday Sedan was built late in the 1955 model year and crashed on May 24, 1956. Notice the word "Holiday" in chrome script on the front fender. Versions of this car built early in the model run had "Super 88" front fender badges, rather than the Holiday script. Super 88s used the same 324-cid/202-hp Rocket V-8 as the big Ninety-Eight model, making them what you might call "factory hot rods."

This 1955 Plymouth Savoy V-8 two-door sedan was only three years of age when this banger took place on March 8, 1958. Plymouth built quite a few of these cars — 74,880 to be exact. The V-shaped emblem on the hood tells us the 241-cid/157-hp Plymouth "Hy-Fire" V-8 is below. Did you notice the GMC fire truck?

"Lucky Seven" reads the sign behind the 1955 Pontiac Star Chief Custom Catalina, but the owner was definitely unlucky. The car wears a license plate frame from Whittier Community Motors, a Pontiac dealership in Whittier, California. This dealership still exists today at 13839 Whittier Boulevard, but it is now known as Community Pontiac. The other car involved in the accident is a much rarer 1961 Chrysler Newport station wagon.

Bayshore Tractor & Equipment Company, which sold Ferguson tractors, was where this 1956 Cadillac wound up after it was involved in an accident with a Divco milk truck and a Peterbilt tractor-trailer near the city limits in Redwood City, California. A little digging reveals that Bayshore Tractor & Equipment was located on Bayshore Road in Palo Alto. The date of the three-vehicle crash was June 19, 1958.

A dapper policeman stands watch over a damaged 1956 Chevy Bel Air convertible after an accident that took place on May 21, 1959. As you can see, the car met an immovable object, but from the looks of the dent in the left front fender it was pushed into this position after an impact with a movable one.

The warning sign says "Stop Ahead," but the owner of the 1956 Chevrolet Bel Air two-door hardtop obviously didn't heed the warning. The V-8 powered Chevy took a dive into a big hole in the road. There was no cell phone use to blame for this June 13, 1960 accident. The smile on the policeman's face seems to suggest that no one was seriously hurt in this mishap. The car seems to be missing its rear fender script and logo badge.

That's a hefty chunk of telephone pole lying in the roadway near a mangled 1956 Chevy Bel Air Sports Sedan. This accident photo is dated February 2, 1959. The dual exhaust pipes on the Classic Chevy indicate that it has the "Power Pack" V-8 with a four-jet carburetor and twin tailpipes. Accident investigators are doing a bit of measuring to try to determine the speed the car was traveling at when the crash happened.

The porthole style hardtop tells us this is a 1956 Thunderbird – or at least it used to be. A fat pole with a fire alarm box mounted on it has "modified" the car's front end quite a bit. In 1956, the second-year "T-Bird" carried a sticker price of $3,151 and Ford sold 15,631 of them. When this accident occurred on October 27, 1963 the pioneering American sports car was worth less than $1,500.

This 1956 Chevy Bel Air Sport Sedan crashed at an intersection in a residential neighborhood on May 4, 1957. The V-shaped badge under the Chevy emblem on front of the hood indicates it has the 265-cid small-block V-8, which was Chevy's only V-8 in 1956. This four-door hardtop was a brand new Chevy model in 1956 and quite popular. A total of 137,672 were built with all engines. The base V-8 version listed for $2,464.

No matter what it looks like, these convertibles aren't "kissing cousins." The one on the left came from Ford of Dearborn, Michigan, while the one on the right is from Oldsmobile of Lansing. One of 49,986 Sunliners made in 1956, the Ford was only worth $700 at the time of the accident on June 22, 1961. The 1960 Olds 98 ragtop is a bit newer and rarer with 7,284 built. It was worth about $3,295 when it was damaged.

This fender-skirted 1956 Ford Fairlane four-door sedan tried to "hedge all bets" after banging into a 1959 Pontiac station wagon on April 25, 1960. The Ford driver did some trick driving to avoid running over a small tree and wound up wedged into the hedge. The Ford suffered some moderate front end damage and did a number all along the passenger side of the Pontiac.

Someone at Tri-City Blueprint & Supply was very unlucky. They waited 25 years for this wonderful car, only to see it get crashed up in a fender bender. It is a model that you didn't see every day in the United States – a 1956 Goliath GP700 limousine. Goliath was a German automaker and German car companies used the term "limousine" to identify sedans. This one is of the two-door variety. The accident occurred October 13, 1959.

On October 23, 1960 this accident sent glass and small car parts flying all over. The car that got hit was a British-built 1956 Hillman Minx convertible. The car's passenger side door window is completely gone, frame and all. It's doubtful that many cars like this one ever made it to the United States. In the background are a police Harley, a vintage Shell gas station and a plain-Jane, tailfinned Rambler.

Members of the Menlo Park Fire Department work to put out a fire under the hood of a 1956 Mercury that crashed into a telephone pole on February 23, 1956. The Mercury two-door hardtop was nearly new at the time. Sgt. Joseph Ferrieva, of the Menlo Park Police Department is busy helping two female motorists who remained in the vehicle during the fire suppression work.

A 1956 Plymouth sedan managed to get wedged in a culvert lined with sandbags. The incident drew a big group of spectators.

Looking a bit like a new hire on her first day on the job at a travel agency, this 1956 Oldsmobile did a bit more damage to the office than you see at first glance. The car appears to have smashed through the window and "re-arranged" the furniture a bit. This crash happened on June 3, 1963. In addition to the car itself, office items like the dial phones and typewriter are collector's items now.

In the late 1950s, the German branch of GM made an economical mid-range Opel Rekord. This one didn't stay on the road for long.

Maybe the letters on the license plate mean "unrestored!" And it's very likely that this 1961 Chevrolet Impala four-door hardtop stayed that way after its accident on June 13, 1962. The heavy rear end damage would be too expensive to repair at reasonable cost. Though many sources indicate deluxe wheel discs were a standard part of the Impala trim package, this one has small "dog dish" hubcaps. It does, however, have an optional V-8 engine.

In this April 5, 1961 crash a 1959 Thunderbird hardtop hit a 1956 Volkswagen Beetle and knocked the small German automobile on its side. According to its front license plate frame, the "Vee-Dub" came from Anderson Volkswagen San Jose, California. The 1959 model was one of the "Squarebird" T-Birds and the hardtop sold for $3,696. This one was still worth $3,180 when the wreck occurred. By contrast the sunroof-equipped VW was worth $735.

Here is another view of the run in between a 1956 Volkswagen sunroof sedan and a 1959 Ford Thunderbird. The Palo Alto Fire Department responded to the scene with its trusty old open-cab pumper, which appears to be a 1930s or early-1940s model. A sign behind the two men standing next to the T-Bird points the way to Stanford Medical center and Palo Alto Stanford Medical center. Note the Standard Oil station.

The leaves of brown came tumbling down that December! The exact date was December 17, 1960 and the hood of a four-year-old Pontiac was where they landed. This car actually knocked the leaves out of the tree after colliding with a 1960 Chevrolet and sliding into the tree. From the shape and condition of the raised trunk lid, viewable through the car's rear window, the Chevrolet first hit the Pontiac in the rear.

The shiny Triumph TR-3 roadster was no match for the unyielding street signpost. Scenes like this sent designers back to the drawing board to offer breakaway supports. Note the mid-1950s GMC service truck (left) and the Mercedes sedan parked across the street.

Oh, please save me that beautiful "California" grille for my 1957 Buick Century sedan. This car is one of 17,029 Buick Century Riviera two-door hardtops made. The car came from Spencer Buick, a dealership located in San Francisco. The travel sticker on its wraparound windshield indicates that it made at least one trip to Canada before it was smashed up in this accident on May 21, 1959. The crash backed up traffic a bit.

The 1957 Chevrolet Bel Air convertible has become an icon of the '50s, but this example might have been long gone by the time people started collecting these cars. This V-8 version is one of 47,562 made. When new, seven years earlier, it went out the dealership door for $2,611. At the time of this crash on August 13, 1964, the average value of this car had dropped to about $450.

Here's a one-year-old 1957 Eldorado Seville again. This view shows that the accident damage extended to the front end of the car, as well as the left-hand side. Even the right door suffered a crinkle from the frontal impact and both right-hand tires were flattened. According to industry guides of the day, this limited-production Cadillac model had an average retail value between $4,185 and $4,290 at the time of the crash.

A huge overpass support proved to be the ultimate immovable object for this late-1960s Pontiac Grand Prix coupe. The car somehow got between the two guardrails bordering either side of the divided highway before plowing into the cement structure.

Many crunched classic Chevys didn't get fixed and we'll almost guarantee that this was one of them. The 1957 Bel Air two-door hardtop looks like it had the engine ripped right out of it. Ironically, something just beyond the tow truck boom — probably another truck —has the word "Lucky" written on it, but it's clear that no one was lucky to be involved in a brutal accident like this June 2, 1958 wreck.

Tail fins on cars and travel trailers were both popular items in 1961, when this crash occurred. The date was May 8, so the owner of the travel trailer may have been heading off on a what seemed like a carefree vacation when disaster struck. In any case, the 1957 Dodge Custom Royal four-door hardtop took the worst of it. In addition to the hood and frontal damage, if you look close you'll see that the car's right-hand fin is bent out of shape.

No crops

A 1957 Chevy cop car purchased from E-Z Davies in Redwood City, California had an accident with a 1949 Dodge on May 22, 1958. The Redwood City police Department put the Chevy 150 four-door sedan into service. Though it's a basic model with "bottle cap" hubcaps, the car uses the hot small-block Chevy V-8 — as indicated by the big "V" hood emblem. The pipe-smoking Dodge owner doesn't look too happy. Would you?

What was once an aluminum-framed quarter window on this rare Fiat Abarth Zagato 750GT "Double Bubble" coupe indicates that it's a very early (circa 1957) competition coupe that somehow rolled over. The body of the car was built of aluminum to keep its track weight down to just 1,250 lbs. Power came from a 747-cc/47-hp engine. A car like this would be exceptionally valuable in today's collector car market and was a desirable piece on November 1, 1959 when it crashed.

A 1955 Imperial sedan, with its distinctive high-mounted tail lights, balances precariously on a curb after smashing into a Chevy van. As banged up as the Imperial is, the smoldering van may have gotten the worst of this exchange.

This pile of parts used to be a proud 1955 Chrysler Imperial with air conditioning, which was a pretty rare option in 1955. Only 7,840 of these Series C69 sedans were built and they sold for $4,483. A 331.1-cid/250-hp Firepower Hemi V-8 lies under that bent-in-half hood. This car was struck by a van on March 25, 1972. Too bad! If it had survived just a few more years, until the old-car hobby boomed in the late '70s, it surely would have wound up with a collector.

This 1957 Lincoln Premiere two-door hardtop. It sold for $5,149 when it was new and 15,185 were manufactured. This one was pretty badly banged up in the March 8, 1957 crash.

A business named Peninsula British Cars appears in the background of numerous photos in the Rodman Bingham Collection. We're betting the car lot in back of this wreck is the same one, though we can't prove it. The crashed car is a 1954 Chevrolet Bel Air sport coupe with an accessory spotlight. It seems to have suffered the most in this fender (and grille) bender, but there are a few signs of damage to the '57 Ford ahead of it as well.

The face of this 1954 Chevrolet Bel Air two-door sedan is twisted and contorted after an accident that took place on August 7, 1955. The Chevy was only a year old at the time.

We've seen "drive-in" eateries, but this one might be called a "drop-down" restaurant. It is not known if the Chevy Bel Air convertible whacked the building before the roof caved in, or whether the car's owner just picked a bad spot to park. Other cars in the photo range from a '41 Cadillac convertible sedan, to an MGA roadster, to a 1953 Pontiac four-door sedan.

Following a damaging crash, a tow truck carried this 1954 Ford Mainline Tudor sedan away. The car was just a year old when this collision happened on June 1, 1955. Front end damage like this dates back to the days when a car's only "crumple zone" was the driver's thorax. This bulky car sold for just $1,651 when it was new, but it was worth lots less in this condition and probably wasn't repaired.

The driver of this 1954 Mercury Custom two-door hardtop (right) somehow didn't see this 1952 Chevrolet coming. From this view, at least, it appears that the older car escaped serious injury, though the sporty Merc is pretty banged up. The man in the white shirt and hat is smoking a cigarette while standing near a fluid spill. We're not sure that's a good idea.

A 1955 Dodge Royal lies upside down following an October 1955 accident on what appears to be a quiet suburban street.

On May 14, 1960 this 1954 Oldsmobile 88 four-door sedan had a date with destiny. Dishing out the damage to the car's right side was a brand new Pontiac Catalina Vista Sedan. This Oldsmobile had an average retail value of only $465 when the crash occurred. Passing behind the Olds is a two-tone 1956 Rambler. There is also a cool old tile-roofed Shell gas station back behind both cars.

"Keep right – except to crash!" Possibly the driver of this 1954 Plymouth Savoy ignored such advice and the sign next to the car. We don't know that for sure, but we can see that the car definitely ran into something that did extensive damage to its front-end sheet metal. The other car was a '56 Ford sporting a custom paint job. The accident dates to March 10, 1956. From the cowl section back, the car appears to be in pretty good shape.

Was an inflatable duck really driving the Buick when it collided with this big Chevy truck? We can only hope so.

This 1955 T-Bird had its removable hardtop taken off the hard way. The beautiful bird was less than a year old when it reached the end of the trail in January of 1956.

These two men were the first motorists on the scene after a 1954 Chevy took a nosedive into a large culvert in February of 1957.

Jumping right on the problem at hand, the tower gets the bumpers of these two cars separated. In the '50s, bumper snags like this were common. From this view, we can also see that the 1954 Pontiac Star Chief has a snazzy custom two-tone paint job and the Studebaker has the S-within-a-circle emblem that indicates it is a Champion Six coupe.

Buick fights tree and gets punched in the nose! We're not much on tree identification, but this car is a 1955 Buick Special two-door hardtop. The sheriff's department officers are left with the thankless job of figuring out what happened, picking up the pieces and writing the whole thing up in an incident report.

Chains and chaining techniques are important tools of vehicle-recovery experts and this fellow (reminds you of Humphrey Bogart, doesn't he?) seems to really know what he's doing. The car appears to be a 1954-1955 Beetle sedan with the optional sliding canvas roof. According to the license plate tag, it came from San Carlos Volkswagen.

Here we see a previously beautiful 1955 Buick Roadmaster sport coupe that was crunched on April 10, 1955. The license plate frame indicates this near-new car was sold by Carl Haas Buick. The new car smell probably hadn't even worn off before this car had to go into the shop for major repairs.

According to the billboard, a boy could slam more homers if he ate Kilpatrick Bread. But no one felt like a home run hitter when this 1955 Buick Super Riviera hardtop slammed into a tiny 1948 Studebaker Champion Regal Deluxe coupe. Considering the relative size and weight of the two machines, one might expect the Studebaker to look much worse than the Buick, but both cars came out pretty even overall.

It's sad to see a rare car wrecked, but it happens. This 1955 Buick Roadmaster convertible coupe was one of just 4,730 ever built. It originally sold for $3,552 and tipped the scales at 4,415 lbs. This same major highway in Menlo Park, California can be seen in a photo of a 1950 Cadillac shown earlier in this book. Codes on back of the photos indicate that both cars were involved in the same collision. Note the Kelsey-Hayes wire wheels on the Buick.

It's hard to tell if this is the front or the back of this poor old Plymouth after it took a heavy blow on a busy highway. Judging from the scorched and peeling paint, the car went up in flames at least briefly after the mishap.

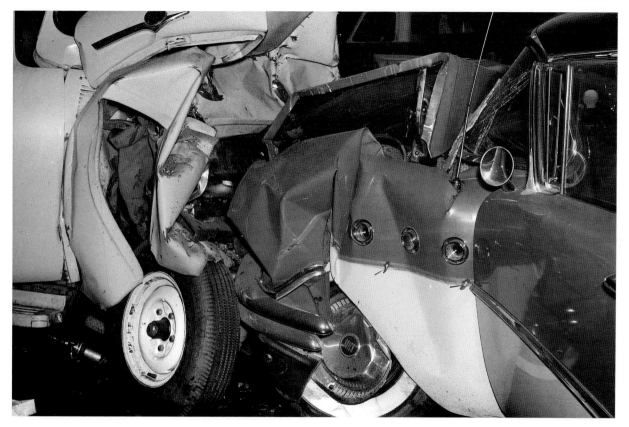

A big old Buick and a Ford truck went nose to nose in June of 1958. These were two pretty sturdy vehicles, but both were destined for the boneyard after this rough collision.

The gouges on the pavement show how this once-proud Oldsmobile was shoved off the tracks after getting in a train's way in the summer of 1957.

A second view of this wreck shows the impact the Olds took on the driver's side. Somehow, the train signal was spared in this horrific incident.

Here's one it really hurts to see … a '55 Chevy Bel Air convertible damaged so badly that it was certainly a "total." The crash took place on the 1300 block of Marsh Road next to Sonny Jim's Eats on June 1, 1955. That means the car was virtually new. It looks like it even had a continental tire kit that got ripped off the rear bumper. Sonny Jim sold Royal Crown Cola, ice cream and Mason's Old Root Beer. It was open all night and ready to serve breakfast, too.

A 1950 Chevrolet Styleline Deluxe takes an offbeat parking spot. A few bricks were crushed, the windows were smashed, several toys were broken, a parking meter post was snapped off, and the Chevy received moderate damage. (Rusty Herlocher photo)

This 1955 Chrysler New Yorker four-door sedan was badly battered in a crash that took place on May 24, 1961. It crunched both front fenders, bent the hood, smashed the grille and twisted the front bumper. Since the car's "book value" at the time of the wreck was $375, it more than likely wound up in the boneyard.

It's pretty easy to pinpoint the location of this crash by the neon sign in the background. It took place March 22, 1957 in Redwood City, California. The Ford Fairlane 500 two-door hardtop was nearly brand new. Even the 1951 Chevy was in pretty nice shape — up to the point of impact. The Yellow Cab sign showing over the roof may be attached to a Checker, judging from what we can see through the Ford's windows.

A police officer inspects a 1951 Ford convertible following an accident. Collectors often like to restore cars found "in the weeds."
This Ford is buried "in the woods." The driver apparently had two spare tires in the trunk.

Now lacking a hood, windshield and backlite, this 1955 Dodge Royal Lancer two-door hardtop looks like the loser in a spin-the-bottle duel. The term Lancer identified Dodge's two-door hardtop and 25,831 were made for the model year. This one was a near-new car, as the photo is dated October 13, 1955. When it left the showroom months, weeks or days earlier, this car went out the door for $2,370.

Somehow, this log truck driver managed to keep from rolling his rig after getting hooked up with a Packard on a tight, tree-lined road in April of 1959.

A second view of this wreckage shows how the two vehicles skidded together off the road. The good news is that it looks like both drivers were able to walk away from an accident that could have been much worse.

This '59 Ford pickup was still looking shiny and new until a tree got in its way in May of 1960. This work truck had a roof-mounted spotlight and what appears to be another spotlight on the box.

"Stop" it says on the road, in big letters, but someone didn't stop fast enough to avoid hitting a 1952 Chevrolet Styleline Special two-door sedan that belonged to a San Francisco newspaper known as the Call-Bulletin. The 1953 Mercury smashed the Chevy's left rear fender and the '55 Dodge Custom Royal Lancer hit the Mercury. The script on the fender of the Dodge reads "Royal Lancer." If it was a Custom Royal Lancer it would say only "Royal."

This '55 Ford Country Sedan station wagon looks like it impaled itself during this crash. One fence post seems to have spiked right through the hood, although it's more likely just a broken piece sitting on the hood. The six-cylinder Country Sedan sold for $2,256 and 53,075 were made. The V-8 version cost $131 additional and 53,209 were made. This accident took place May 2, 1956 when the car was just one year old and still had lots of value.

The 1955 Thunderbird was an automotive sensation in 1955. Seeing one driving on the street was enough to draw a big crowd. Seeing one up ended in a crash was a far less common sight. With a steep-for-the-time base price of $2,944, most owners were pretty careful when tooling around in a T-Bird, but as we all know, accidents happen. This one took place on Halloween night in 1955, so the car was no more than a year old.

How did this '55 Olds Super 88 Holiday Sedan get to the bottom of this pool? Probably not through the gate. Amazingly, the pool and car look in remarkably good shape.